SO YOU'RE

50!

Mike Haskins & Clive Whichelow

Illustrations by Andy Hammond

summersdale

SO YOU'RE 50!

First published in 2007
Second edition published in 2008
This edition copyright © Mike Haskins and Clive Whichelow, 2013

Illustrations by Andy Hammond

Summersdale Publishers Ltd
46 West Street
Chichester
West Sussex
PO19 1RP
UK

www.summersdale.com

Printed and bound in China

ISBN: 978-1-84953-438-3

Substantial discounts on bulk quantities of Summersdale books are available to corporations, professional associations and other organisations. For details contact Nicky Douglas by telephone: +44 (0) 1243 756902, fax: +44 (0) 1243 786300 or email: nicky@summersdale.com.

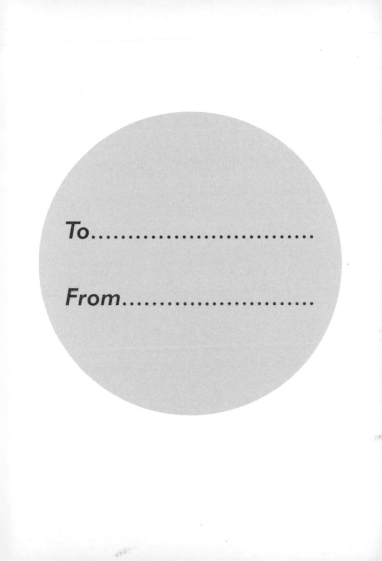

To...............................

From.........................

INTRODUCTION

So you've done it! You've reached another of life's milestones. You've reached the age you never thought you'd reach. And it isn't even the first age you never thought you'd reach that you've reached. It's probably something like the third or fourth.

And here it is. The big one: 50. It's a wonder the shock of it hasn't killed you. Especially at your age. You can't argue with people who call you middle-aged any more. Oh yes, you tried to deny it throughout your decade as a giddy young 40-something. But in your 50s, you have no defence.

Thankfully, this little volume will help you adjust. Sit awhile, relax and think on the *many rich mysteries with which life has presented you. Such as why, when you have spent every last hard-earned penny raising and educating your kids and imparted your worldly wisdom to them, they have grown up into people with whom you have nothing in common whatsoever?*

Well, we can ponder these things, but there probably aren't any answers.

THE BASIC MYTHS ABOUT TURNING 50

50 is the new 40 –
it's not

Saga holidays are the new 18 to 30 – no they're not, but they do involve going on holiday with a bunch of people who look like they were born in 1830

DRESS CODE FOR THE OVER 50S – SOME DOS & DON'TS

Don't try to look younger by body piercing – it will just look like you had a really horrible accident while doing some DIY

Do cover up your midriff or it will look like you're carrying an airbag made of lard

*Don't dress in a tracksuit
and bling as you will now
look less like a badass
rapper and more like
Ozzy Osbourne*

Don't even think about a thong

HOW TO APPEAR YOUNGER THAN YOU ACTUALLY ARE

Hang around with people even older than you are (e.g. if possible join The Rolling Stones)

Swap the car for a moped with an L-plate

*Learn to sit down
without saying 'Aah,
that's better'*

Wear your baseball cap back to front

A GUIDE TO HOW OTHERS WILL NOW PERCEIVE YOU

As a health insurance risk

As a reactionary old git

THE MAIN EVENTS IN YOUR LIFE YOU CAN NOW LOOK FORWARD TO

A second honeymoon – and being able to get out to see the sights this time

Having a beautiful set of white teeth which are not only all new but removable for easy cleaning

THE MAIN
EVENTS IN YOUR
LIFE THAT ARE
LESS EASY TO
LOOK FORWARD
TO

Becoming a grandparent
before you're mentally
attuned to the idea

*Losing brain cells –
then again if you
lose enough, you
won't notice*

The first time you get out of breath running up the stairs

CONVERSING WITH YOUNG PEOPLE (PART 1)

*What you say and
what they hear*

*'How are you getting on
at university?' =
'Are you on drugs?'*

'Have you got a boyfriend/
girlfriend yet?' =
'Are you gay?'

'We didn't use to bother with sell-by dates in my day' = 'Scrape the mould off the bread and stop whinging'

A LIST OF CONTROVERSIAL OPINIONS YOU WILL NOW BE EXPECTED TO HOLD

'Being unemployed should be against the law'

'Not only does capital
punishment have a lot going
for it, it should be introduced
for all motoring offences'

CONVERSING WITH YOUNG PEOPLE (PART 2)

*What they say and
what you hear*

*'Is it all right if I stay over
with a friend tonight?'* =
'I am going to an orgy'

*'I'm moving out and getting
a place of my own'* =
'I'll be back Saturday'

*'I'm thinking of
getting married'* =
'There's a baby on the way'

THINGS YOU CAN NOW GET AWAY WITH THAT YOU COULDN'T PREVIOUSLY

Being obsessed with gardening

Buying £3 supermarket jeans – and maybe even wearing them

THINGS YOU ARE NOW LIKELY TO HAVE IN YOUR HOME

A Neighbourhood Watch sticker in your window

A smoke alarm that actually works – particularly when you make toast

Proper framed pictures (posters don't count!)

THINGS
THAT YOU WILL
TAKE A SUDDEN
INTEREST IN

Newspaper articles on heart attack warning signs

Other people's operations

Pension annuity levels

Loyalty card points

THINGS YOU'LL NEVER HAVE TO DO AGAIN

Change a nappy – until the grandchildren arrive that is

Explain how babies are made

BOO! THINGS YOU WON'T BE DOING AGAIN

Having a wide
choice of hairstyles

Painting a white stripe down the side of your Ford Cortina to make yourself look like Starsky and Hutch

Being asked to turn the noise down

SHATTERING MOMENTS TO COME SOON

Your first pair
of bifocals

*When you wake up with
a terrible hangover and
remember you didn't have a
drink the night before*

Walking down the high street and seeing an individual who is clearly mutton dressed as lamb only to then realise it's your own reflection in a shop window

THINGS TO EXPECT FOR YOUR NEXT BIRTHDAY

*A tin of biscuits
in a little pack
with a small jar of
strawberry jam*

A specially arranged surprise reunion with people you hoped never to see again

BEING 50 IS...

... being too old for basketball but too young for bowls

... *being too old for a trendy haircut but too young for a hairpiece*

YOUR NEW
OUTLOOK
ON LIFE

Your idea of a dirty weekend is clearing out the garden shed

Your idea of life in the fast lane is queuing at the 'Five items or fewer' checkout in the supermarket

*Your idea of a busy
weekend is doing
the shopping and
washing the car*

*Your idea of a sensual
massage is provided by one
of those big vibrating blue
sock things you stick your
feet in and plug into
the mains*

YOUR NEW
WEEKLY
HIGHLIGHTS

Having a chat with the milkman

*The local newspaper
printing your latest
letter complaining
about something*

For ladies, the weekly exercise workout in the church hall; for men, walking past and peering through the window of the church hall while the ladies' weekly exercise workout is in full swing

REASONS TO
BE CHEERFUL

*In a hostage situation
you are likely to be
released first*

You're now old enough to have a toy boy/girl

If you're interested in finding out more about our books, find us on Facebook at Summersdale Publishers and follow us on Twitter at @Summersdale.

www.summersdale.com